**W9-ALM-512**

WORD BIRD'S VALENTINE WORDS

by Jane Belk Moncure
illustrated by Sue Mead Fullam
Creative Studios I, Inc.

Created by

THE
CHILD'S
WORLD

Distributed by CHILDRENS PRESS ®
Chicago, Illinois

CHILDRENS PRESS HARDCOVER EDITION
ISBN 0-516-06578-5

CHILDRENS PRESS PAPERBACK EDITION
ISBN 0-516-46578-3

Library of Congress Cataloging in Publication Data

Moncure, Jane Belk.
  Word Bird's Valentine words.

  (Word house words for early birds)
  Summary: Word Bird makes a Valentine Word House, in
which he puts special words related to that season.
Illustrations help the reader define the words introduced.
    1. Vocabulary—Juvenile literature.   2. Saint
Valentine's Day—Juvenile literature.   [1. Vocabulary.
2. Valentine's Day]   I. Fullam, Sue Mead, ill.   II. Title.
III. Series: Moncure, Jane Belk.   Word house words for
early birds.
PE1449.M5338   1987   428.1   87-13785
ISBN 0-89565-362-1

1 2 3 4 5 6 7 8 9 10 11 12 R 95 94 93 92 91 90 89 88 87

WORD BIRD'S
VALENTINE WORDS

Word Bird made a...

word house.

"I will put valentine
words in my house,"
he said.

He put in these words—

February 14

Valentine's Day

paper hearts

9

hug   kiss
sweetheart
Be mine.
I love you.

valentine words

valentines

valentine tree

Roses are red.
Violets are blue.
Sugar is Sweet.
And so are you.

valentine verse

valentine post office

valentine puppets

valentine hats

love

I love you

Come
Valen
Par

King of Hearts

hug

Be mine

to our
ine
ty

Queen of Hearts

candy hearts

pink lemonade

Valentine's Day party

valentine mail

"I love you."

Can you read thes

Valentine's Day

valentine tree

February 14

valentine verse

paper hearts

valentine post office

valentine words

Hugs love

valentine puppets

valentines

valentine hats

...alentine words with Word Bird?

King of
Hearts

Valentine's Day
party

Queen of
Hearts

valentine
mail

candy
hearts

"I
love
you."

pink
lemonade

You can make a valentine word house. You can put Word Bird's words in your house and read them too.

Can you think of other Valentine words to put in your word house?